A LITTLE
BOOK OF
English
· TEAS ·

ROSA MASHITER

Illustrated by MILANDA LOPEZ

D0966107

First published in 1989 by
The Appletree Press Ltd, 19–21 Alfred Street,
Belfast BT2 8DL
Tel. +44 (0) 1232 243074
Fax +44 (0) 1232 246756
Text © Rosa Mashiter, 1989
Illustrations © Milanda Lopez, 1989
Printed in the E.U. All rights reserved.

A Little Book of English Teas

First published in the United States in 1989 by
Chronicle Books, 275 Fifth Street,
San Francisco, CA 94103

ISBN 0-8118-1011-9

9 8 7 6 5 4 3 2 1

Introduction

There are a number of legends about the origins of tea but the most probable is that concerning Emperor Shen Nung, an early Chinese hygienist, who discovered that the boiling of water made it safe to drink. Legend says that, as he boiled his water out in the open one day, the leaves from a nearby tree fell into the boiling cauldron and so he invented tea. This occurred in 2737 B.C.

Gradually the Chinese took the tea plant (*Camellia Sinensis*) to many parts of China and, like wine, the quality varied according to the soil and climate in which the tea was grown. The Chinese tea ceremony evolved over many years with three types of tea being used, Green, Red (Oolong), and Black, and the Chinese became so enamored with tea that at one point there was a law forbidding the export of tea from China. This is probably why the Western world did not hear about tea until comparatively recent times.

Those great navigators, the Portuguese, were the first to bring tea to Europe, and it was the Portuguese Princess Catherine of Braganza who brought the first tea to Britain in her royal dowry when she married Charles II in 1662. While coffee had come to Britain earlier and was well established, tea began with a bad reception. The clergy of the time said that since it came from a heathen country it was a sinful drink and doctors agreed that it was unhealthy. Brewers lobbied the government, complaining that tea might replace ale at breakfast. This provided a wonderful excuse for the government to tax tea, and in 1689 they did, putting five shillings tax per pound on dry leaf, making tea prohibitively expensive overnight.

In 1706, a young tea merchant named Thomas Twining bought an existing coffee house called "Tom's" just off London's Strand, close to where the aristocracy was building new homes after the

Great Fire of London in 1664. Twining was very aware that coffee houses needed to specialize to draw customers for the competition was tremendous; there were some 2500 coffee houses in London alone. After ten years' trading as a coffee house specializing in good quality tea, he knew that the ladies of the aristocracy were the people most likely to buy his tea, and he knew no lady would enter a coffee house. So he bought three small houses and turned them into a shop in 1717. This was probably the first dry tea and coffee shop in Britain and, indeed, the Western world. It was also a place where a lady could enter without impropriety.

If a lady could afford to buy tea from Thomas Twining (the most reasonable was Green Gunpowder at 16 shillings per pound) she could certainly afford to have a craftsman make a small chest in which to keep it. Later, these developed into more elaborate tea caddies. Caddies always had a lock and key and two compartments, for green and black tea. Quite often there was also a mixing bowl, in which some ladies kept their sugar, another expensive item. Tea was treated like gold dust and the lady of the house kept the key of the caddy on her belt, offering this precious commodity only to very important visitors. She herself presided over the boiling of the water, the measuring of the dry leaves with a caddy spoon, and the making and serving of the tea. That is how the British tea ceremony started.

The lady of the house used a small china teapot and bowls, all imported from China, and when British potters started to make teapots they were still small, as tea was so expensive. Later, as tea became more affordable, teapots became bigger, but it was not until 1784 that tea truly arrived. That was the year in which Richard Twining, grandson of Thomas Twining, and Chairman of the tea dealers' guild, persuaded William Pitt to reduce the tax on tea, making Britain the nation of tea drinkers it is today.

At that time all tea came from China. Teapots grew larger and

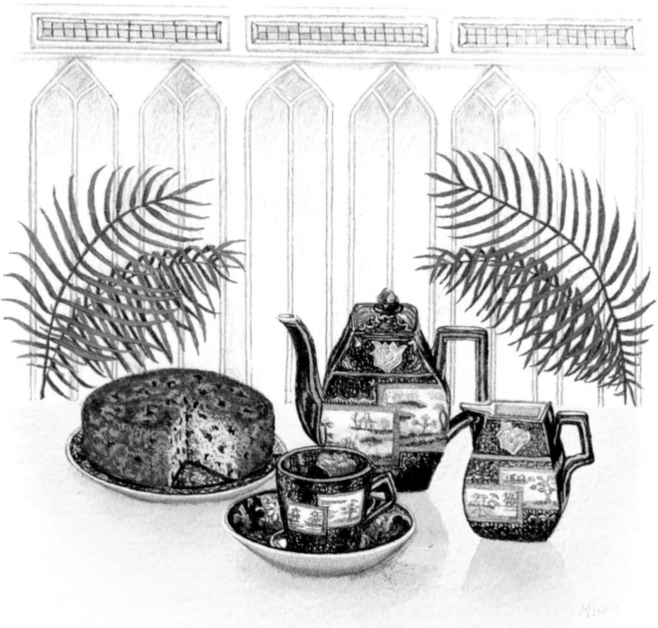

more ornate as Britain entered an age of elegance and social life changed. And when, in the late eighteenth century, afternoon tea started to emerge as a meal, the lady of the house presided over the table as she still does to this day. The seventh Duchess of Bedford is credited with having invented afternoon tea, and certainly it became very fashionable in late Georgian and early Victorian times. Craftsmen responded to the demand and all the lovely things we associate with afternoon tea stem from that period.

The first Indian tea arrived in 1839 and, coming from a British colony, was allowed in without duty. Ceylon tea followed in 1879 and received the same favorable treatment. The market for china tea suffered a good deal, but never disappeared completely.

Afternoon tea, which is enjoying a great revival today, can be served any time from 3:00 PM to 5:30 P.M. It is still correct for the hostess to make and pour the tea. If two different teas are being offered, the most important of the lady guests is asked to pour the second pot. One tea will most likely be Earl Grey (named after the Prime Minister of 1835) and the other probably a Darjeeling tea from the foothills of the Indian Himalayas. Milk must always be offered, but never cream, and if milk is taken, it should always be put in the cup first. Sliced lemon should be available and white sugar should be on the table for those who desire it. One of the many good points about afternoon tea is that the food varies with the seasons: thin sandwiches with cucumber, lettuce, tomato in the summer, jam and meat paste in the winter.

Similarly, the cakes in the summer will be light and creamy, in the winter, heavier, spicier and fruity. There are no strict rules governing afternoon tea, you can look at the food, pick at the food, or make a pig of yourself; no one minds.

Teas to drink with all these delicious foods can change according to your mood, the weather, the food and the company you keep.

Here are some suggestions: for a hot day, Lapsang Souchong from Fujian Province of China served with cucumber sandwiches; for a warm day, Earl Grey scented with the oil of Bergamot; or Ceylon tea, a golden liquor that is delicious with a slice of lemon. On a colder day, try a tea with more body, such as Darjeeling; or Keemun, from the Chinese province of Anhui. In really cold weather, try Indian Assam, the marvelously malty pungent tea which goes so well with milk.

There is a tea for everyone, so it pays to experiment and never hold back in making your own blend. Two or three teaspoonsful of Assam and one teaspoon of Earl Grey allows a lovely nuance to come through; or Ceylon with a faint trace of Lapsang Souchong. There are many combinations you can try. Have fun and tease the palates of your guests at tea time.

Samuel Twining

English Tea-Time Sandwich

Invented by the Earl of Sandwich in the eighteenth century, the English tea-time sandwich has become a well-established tradition.

It is far better to use bread that is a day old, for to create the really elegant English tea-time sandwich it is necessary to use very thinly sliced bread – either white or brown, and to remove crusts once the sandwiches have been filled.

Cucumber Sandwiches

It is necessary to sweat the cucumber beforehand to avoid ending up with soggy sandwiches.

---

cucumber
vinegar
salt
thinly sliced bread
butter

Peel and very thinly slice some cucumber, put the slices into a colander sitting on a deep plate, sprinkle a little vinegar and some salt all over and leave for 30–40 minutes. Shake the colander to remove any excess liquid and pat the cucumber slices dry with paper towels.

Lightly butter the bread, arrange an overlapping layer of cucumber on top, cover with another slice of lightly buttered bread, and press the two together firmly. Trim off the crusts with a sharp knife and cut the sandwich into four triangles. Pile neatly onto a place covered with a lacy doily, and serve at once.

Egg and Watercress Sandwiches

2 hard-boiled eggs	softened butter
1 tsp mayonnaise	thinly sliced bread
salt and pepper	watercress

Peel the eggs and chop roughly into a food processor, then add the mayonnaise, and some of the cress snipped off with scissors. Season with salt and pepper and process to mix (the mixture should have a good texture).

Spread the mixture on some lightly buttered bread, top with another slice, press lightly together, trim off the crusts and cut the sandwich into three fingers. Arrange on a pretty serving plate.

Potted Meat Sandwiches

left-over roast beef	pinch of ground mace
softened butter	thinly sliced white or
salt and freshly ground	brown bread
black pepper	

Finely mince the beef in a food processor and add enough softened butter to bind together. Season with salt and pepper and a pinch of mace. Lightly butter the bread and spread the potted meat in an even, reasonably generous layer. Top with a second slice of bread, press lightly together, trim off the crusts and cut into neat fingers.

Tomato Sandwiches

ripe, but firm tomatoes
thinly sliced, buttered white or brown bread
salt and pepper

Put the tomatoes, stalks removed, into a basin, cover with boiling water, let stand for 1 minute then slide off the skins. Pat dry with paper towels, then cut the tomatoes into thin slices, and arrange on slices of buttered bread. Season with a little salt and pepper, cover with a second slice of bread and press down firmly. Trim off the crusts and cut sandwiches into triangles. Pile neatly onto a serving plate and cover with a slightly dampened dish-towel until ready to serve.

Smoked Salmon Pinwheels

These very elegant little sandwiches should be served for special-occasion teas, such as christenings, birthdays, and weddings.

5 or 6 thin slices of soft brown bread, crusts removed
1 cup low-fat cream cheese
1 1/2 tbsp lemon juice
1 tbsp very finely chopped fresh parsley
1 tbsp very finely chopped watercress
black pepper
pinch cayenne pepper
4 oz smoked salmon slices
lemon twist and watercress to garnish

Using a rolling pin, slightly flatten and stretch the bread. Cream the cheese, lemon juice, parsley, and watercress together, mixing in the seasonings. Spread the mixture evenly over the bread, cover with the slices of smoked salmon and very carefully roll up firmly.

Wrap each roll in foil, or plastic wrap, and refrigerate for at least 2 hours to chill well. Remove the wrapping and cut each roll, using a sharp knife, into 5–6 slices.

To serve, arrange the pinwheels on a fine bone china sandwich plate and garnish with a generous sprig of watercress and a twist of lemon.

Lancashire Cheese Scones

These little scones make a delightful savory, and you can ring the changes by using cheese from different regions, such as Cheddar, Wensleydale, or Cheshire. Serve warm, split, and lightly buttered.

1 1/2 cups self-rising flour	pinch of cayenne pepper
2 tbsp margarine	1 egg
1/2 cup Lancashire cheese, grated	a little milk
pinch of salt	a little beaten egg

Put the flour and margarine into a food processor and process until the mixture resembles coarse breadcrumbs. Add the cheese, salt, and cayenne and mix for just a few seconds. With the machine switched on add the egg, together with just enough milk to make a soft pliable dough. Roll out on a lightly floured board and cut into rounds using a pastry cutter. Place on a greased baking sheet, brush with beaten egg, and bake for about 20 minutes at 425°F.

Devonshire Splits

Traditionally these little buns are served with West Country clotted cream and homemade strawberry jam. Served with a pot of tea this would be called a cream tea in the West Country.

---

4 1/2 cups bread flour
1/2 tsp salt
1 1/4 cups warm milk
1 tsp sugar
2 tsp active dry yeast
2 tbsp melted butter

Sift flour and salt into a mixing bowl. Heat the milk until tepid, stir in the sugar and sprinkle the yeast on top. Leave in a warm place for 15 minutes, by which time it should be frothy. Make a well in the center of the flour, pour in the yeast liquid and melted butter, and using a wooden spoon, mix to a soft dough. Turn onto a floured board and knead for 8–10 minutes. Put in a clean bowl, cover with plastic wrap and leave to stand until doubled in size.

Cut the dough into 12 even-sized pieces, knead each piece into a ball, flatten into a round about 1/2 inch thick and place on a lightly greased and warmed baking sheet. Cover with a cloth and let stand in a warm place for 20 minutes.

Bake at 425°F for 15–20 minutes. Remove from the oven and cool on a wire rack, before splitting and spreading with clotted cream and strawberry jam.

Clotted Cream

It is believed that it was the Phoenicians, in search of tin, who first brought clotted cream to Cornwall, and thence to Devon. The clotted cream from Cornwall varies from the rich, yellow cream of Devon in that it has a delicious buttery yellow crust on top and its consistency is thicker. It is usually made with whole cream (whereas the Devonshire variety is made with creamy milk). A bowl of settled cream is put into a pan of hot water before being scalded. The pan is then removed from the heat and let stand for at least 24 hours in a cool place. The crusty cream will have settled on the top of the pan, and can be easily removed with a large slotted spoon. The skimmed, or buttermilk left below the cream may be put to good use in soups or sauces.

Banana and Walnut Loaf

This is a lovely moist cake that keeps well. It is eaten sliced, with or without butter.

1/2 cup margarine	2 1/4 cups self-rising flour
3/4 cup dark brown sugar	1 tsp baking powder
2 ripe bananas	1/2 cup chopped walnuts
2 eggs	2 tbsp milk

Grease and line a 2-lb loaf pan with parchment paper, and preheat the oven to 350°F. Cream the margarine and sugar together. Mash the bananas and add to the mixture. Break the eggs, one at a time, into the mixture, beating well between each addition. Gently fold in the flour and baking powder and then stir in the walnuts and milk. Transfer the mixture into the loaf pan, smoothing the top, and bake for approximately one hour, or until well risen and golden brown. Turn out and cool on a wire rack.

Almond Biscuits

3/4 cup self-rising flour
1/3 cup butter
1/3 cup ground almonds
1 tbsp superfine sugar
a little milk
a few flaked almonds

Sift the flour into a bowl, and rub the butter in with the fingertips until the mixture resembles fine breadcrumbs. Stir in the ground almonds and sugar, adding a little milk, to form a soft dough.

Roll the dough out on a lightly floured board, to a rectangle about 7 inches square, and place on a greased baking sheet. Brush with a little milk and sprinkle over a few flaked almonds. Bake for 15–20 minutes at 375°F. Remove from the oven and cut immediately into fingers, then allow to cool.

Crumpets

These delicious round "holey" scones are excellent served freshly cooked, spread with butter and jam.

---

2 cups water and milk mixed
1 tbsp active dry yeast
4¹/₂ cups bread flour
1 tsp salt

Heat the water and milk mixture until just tepid and remove from heat. Dissolve the yeast in a little of the warm liquid. Put the flour and salt into a large bowl, make a well in the center, and pour in the yeast and remaining liquid, mixing well with a wooden spoon. Cover the bowl with plastic wrap, and keep in a warm place until the mixture rises (you may need to add a little more warm milk to ensure batter consistency).

Heat a lightly greased cast iron griddle and place greased, metal crumpet rings on top. Spoon in some of the mixture, filling the rings halfway, and cook until bubbles form on the top. Then remove the rings and cook for a couples of minutes further, until the underside is lightly browned.

If you do not have crumpet rings, you can use egg rings, or alternatively spoon the mixture directly onto the griddle. The crumpets will be thinner, but just as delicious.

Northumberland "Singin' Hinny"

These little flat cakes make a "singing" noise as they cook on the griddle. The word "hinny" is a term of endearment usually used by mothers in the north of England. When young children would pester their mothers as to whether their tea was ready or not, and as the little cakes were cooking away, she would answer them by saying, "No, no, they're not ready yet, just singin', hinny."

---

2 1/2 cups self-rising flour
1 tsp salt
4 tbsp lard
4 tbsp superfine sugar
6 tbsp currants
3/4 cup milk and heavy cream mixed

Sift the flour and salt into a large mixing bowl, rub the fat into the flour using your fingertips, and stir in the sugar and currants. Make a well in the center, and pour in the milk and cream mixture. With a wooden spoon slowly draw dry ingredients into the liquid to form a soft dough, finally working with your fingers. Roll the dough out on a lightly floured board to about 1/4 inch thick and prick all over with a fork. Cut into quarters and place on a moderately hot griddle and cook for about 4 minutes each side, until nicely browned. Serve hot, cut in two and buttered.

Florentines

These very elegant and delicious cookies take a little time, but are superb.

---

4 tbsp butter
$^1/_2$ cup dark brown sugar
I egg
$^1/_4$ cup glacé cherries
a few pieces of candied angelica
I cup mixed candied citrus peel
$^1/_2$ cup chopped walnuts
I tbsp sultanas
$^3/_4$ cup dried coconut
4 oz plain dark chocolate

Beat the butter and sugar together and beat in the egg. Roughly chop the glacé cherries and angelica and add to the egg mixture together with the mixed peel, walnuts, sultanas, and coconut. Mix well.

Put teaspoonfuls of the mixture onto a baking sheet which has been covered with lightly greased cooking parchment. Space the spoonfuls reasonably far apart as the cookies will spread out as they cook. Bake at 350°F for about 25 minutes.

Remove from the oven and leave on the baking sheet for about 10 minutes until hard. Carefully transfer to a wire rack to cool.

Melt the chocolate over a bowl of hot water, and drizzle a teaspoonful over each cookie. Allow to set.

Bath Buns

Cobb's, founded by James Cobb in 1866 in Bath, has been making these delectable little buns from an old recipe of 1679 to this day. They are served in the Pump Room at Bath and, with their distinctive sugared top, are a delight not to be missed.

4¹/₂ cups bread flour	³/₄ cup butter
1 tbsp active dry yeast	3 eggs, beaten
1 tsp granulated sugar	¹/₂ cup superfine sugar
pinch salt	crushed sugar cubes for topping
1 cup milk and water mixed	

Put a third of the flour into a large mixing bowl, crumble in the yeast and add 1 teaspoon granulated sugar and a pinch of salt. Heat the water and milk mixture until just tepid and pour over the dry ingredients. Mix well, and leave to stand in a warm place for about ¹/₂ hour. Meanwhile, soften the butter and beat with the eggs until light and creamy. Add to the mixing bowl with the remaining flour and superfine sugar. Turn onto a floured board and knead until smooth, then put into a bowl, cover with plastic wrap, and leave to rise until doubled in size.

When ready, knead again and divide into 15 or 16 slightly flattened balls and place on a greased baking sheet. Cover again and let rise for about 30 minutes. Brush the buns with a little beaten egg and sprinkle the crushed sugar cubes over the top.

Bake at 400°F for 15–20 minutes, or until golden brown. Serve split and buttered.

Maids of Honor

These little tartlets are said to have originated at the court of Henry VIII, when he chanced one day upon some of the Queen's maids of honor eating cakes. Being famous for his voracity, he could not resist the temptation to try a cake himself, and found them so delicious he named them Maids of Honor.

---

8 oz frozen puff pastry, defrosted
1⅓ cups bakers' cheese
6 tbsp softened butter
2 eggs
1 tbsp brandy
2 tbsp superfine sugar
¼ cup ground almonds
pinch of ground nutmeg
a few flaked almonds

Roll the puff pastry out on a lightly floured board and line 12 lightly greased muffin-pan wells with it. Mix together all the remaining ingredients, except the flaked almonds, and spoon into the pastry cases. Sprinkle a few flaked almonds on each and then bake at 425°F for 15–20 minutes until the pastry is golden brown and the filling is set.

Chelsea Buns

A favorite of George III, and so named because they were sold from the Old Chelsea Bun House.

I cup milk and water mixed
2 tsp active dry yeast
3 cups flour
I tsp salt
4 tbsp margarine
$^3/_4$ cup brown sugar
I egg, beaten
2 tbsp butter, melted
I $^1/_2$ cups mixed dried fruit
Glaze:
2 tbsp superfine sugar
4 tbsp boiling water

Heat the milk and water until tepid, sprinkle over the yeast and let stand in a warm place for 20 minutes, by which time it should be frothy. Put the flour and salt into a bowl and rub in the margarine with your fingertips until the mixture resembles fine breadcrumbs. Stir in a third of the brown sugar. Add the milk mixture and beaten egg and mix to form a pliable dough. Turn onto a floured board and knead for 4 minutes, then put into a clean bowl, cover with plastic wrap and let stand until the dough has doubled in size.

Turn onto a floured board, knead again lightly, and roll out to a 20 x 8-inch rectangle. Brush with melted butter, sprinkle with mixed fruit and remaining brown sugar, and roll up from the longest side to form a jelly roll shape. Cut into 12 slices and place cut side down in a deep, lightly greased and warmed pan. Cover

with a cloth and leave in a warm place until doubled in size (about 30 minutes). Bake at 400°F for 20 minutes. Remove from the pan and cool on a rack. Dissolve the sugar in the boiling water and brush all over the top and sides of the buns. Leave to cool completely.

Melting Moments

My late mother-in-law was an excellent baker who enjoyed nothing more than setting a day aside each week to bake an assortment of cakes, biscuits, scones, buns, and bread, and I enjoyed many delicious tea-times with her. Melting Moments, delicious little confections that really do melt in the mouth, were among her favorites.

---

5 tbsp lard
6 tbsp sugar
1 egg
1 1/4 cups self-rising flour
few drops vanilla extract
crushed cornflakes or dried coconut

Cream the fat and sugar together until light and fluffy, then add the egg and beat well. Fold in the flour and vanilla extract. Roll the mixture into small balls the size of walnuts, then roll in crushed cornflakes (or dried coconut). Place on a greased baking sheet and bake for 10 minutes only at 375°F.

Banbury Cakes

When I moved to the West Country many years ago, I found that on visits to my parents, who lived on the Oxfordshire/ Buckinghamshire border, I had to drive through Banbury, famous for its cross and for its little cakes. Sadly, the cake shop I used to visit has long gone but you can still enjoy Banbury Cakes in the local tea shop and in some of the pubs.

---

1 lb frozen puff pastry, defrosted
4 tbsp butter
6 tbsp brown sugar
$^2/_3$ cup currants
1 tbsp rum
$^1/_4$ cup mixed candied citrus peel
$^1/_2$ tsp ground allspice
$^1/_2$ tsp ground cinnamon
beaten egg
superfine sugar

Roll out the pastry on a well-floured board and using a side plate as a guide cut out 6–8 circles. Mix all the remaining ingredients together, except the beaten egg and superfine sugar, and divide equally among the pastry rounds. Dampen all around the edges with water, then draw edges up over the filling and seal in the center; lightly flatten. Place the cakes, seal side down on a greased baking sheet and make three little slits on the top. Bake at 450°F for 20 minutes. Just before the cakes are ready, brush with a little egg and sprinkle over a little sugar, then return to the oven for a few minutes.

Porterhouse Plum Cake

Although called a plum cake, it does not in fact contain plums but nuts and raisins. I find that the addition of grapefruit gives it a distinctive tangy flavor.

$2^2/_3$ cups raisins
4 tbsp water
2 fresh grapefruits
$3^1/_2$ cups self-rising flour
I tsp baking powder
4 tbsp butter
4 tbsp superfine sugar
I cup chopped almonds
3 tbsp milk
2 eggs
superfine sugar for topping

Roughly chop the raisins and put into a pan with the water over a gentle heat.

Squeeze all the juice from one of the grapefruits, and finely grate the rind. Peel the second grapefruit and segment the flesh, removing all the pith and seeds, then roughly chop the flesh.

Put the flour and baking powder into a mixing bowl and rub in the butter. Stir in the sugar and chopped nuts and mix well. Add the raisin mixture, milk, grapefruit juice, and eggs, and mix in the grapefruit rind and flesh.

Pour into a large greased, parchment-lined 8-inch square pan and cook at 350°F for about an hour, or until golden brown. Turn out and cool on a wire rack. Dredge the top with superfine sugar.

Simnel Cake

When young girls went into domestic service, this cake was baked for Mothering Sunday, the only day in the year when they were allowed home. The girls demonstrated the cooking skills they had learned by taking with them a rich fruit cake, decorated with almond paste, called a Simnel Cake. Later the cake became popular at Easter when it was decorated with eleven marzipan balls, symbolizing the faithful disciples, and tied with a satin ribbon.

8 oz marzipan	8 tbsp sultanas
3/4 cup margarine	6 tbsp mixed candied citrus peel
12 tbsp brown sugar	**Decoration:**
4 eggs	1 lb marzipan
1 1/4 cups flour	3 tbsp apricot jam
1 tsp ground cinnamon	1 egg white
2 cups currants	

Line with parchment and lightly grease an 8-inch round cake pan. Roll the 8 oz marzipan to a 7 1/2-inch circle. Cream the margarine and sugar until light and fluffy, then beat in the eggs, one at a time. Put the flour, cinnamon and dried fruit into a large bowl and mix well. Fold half of the dry ingredients into the egg, margarine, and sugar mixture with a metal spoon. When thoroughly mixed, fold in the remaining half. Put half the cake mixture into the pan, and level with a metal spatula knife, then lay the circle of marzipan on the top. Carefully top with the remaining cake mixture, smoothing the top level, then making a shallow well in the center to enable the cake to rise evenly.

Bake at 325°F for 2 hours. When cooked, remove from the pan onto a wire cooling rack and leave the cake to become cold before

decorating.

Divide the marzipan into two pieces. Roll out one half to fit the top of the cake. Roll the other half of marzipan into 11 individual little balls.

To make the decoration, put the apricot jam into a small saucepan and heat gently, then strain through a sieve. Spread over the top of the cake and press the large piece of marzipan firmly on top. Crimp the edges of the marzipan all the way around with thumb and forefinger of your left hand and the forefinger of your right. Lightly beat the egg white and use a little to secure the balls firmly and evenly around the edges of the top of the cake. Then brush all over the top of the cake with egg white and put under a hot broiler for 1–2 minutes, until only the marzipan is well browned.

Jam Tart

1 cup flour
4 tbsp margarine
2 tbsp superfine sugar
water
6 tbsp jam

Put the flour into a large mixing bowl and rub in the margarine, using your fingertips, until the mixture resembles fine breadcrumbs. Stir in the sugar and add enough water to form a firm dough. Roll out on a lightly floured board and use to line an 8-inch flan dish. Spread the jam over the base, and decorate with thin strips of leftover pastry in a lattice design. Bake at 400°F for 30 minutes, until the pastry is golden brown.

Rock Cakes

The mixture is spooned into rough, rocky shapes before baking, hence the name.

---

2 1/4 cups self-rising flour
1/2 cup margarine
1/2 cup superfine sugar
2/3 cup mixed dried fruit
I egg
I tbsp milk

Put the flour and margarine, cut up into small pieces, in a large mixing bowl and, using the fingertips, rub the margarine into the flour until the mixture resembles coarse breadcrumbs. Add the sugar and dried fruit and mix well. Beat the egg and stir it into the mixture together with the milk to make a stiff dough. Spoon the mixture into small rocky-shaped piles on a greased baking sheet.

Bake at 400°F for about 15 minutes until the cakes are golden brown and firm to the touch. Remove from the baking sheet, using a metal spatula knife, and cool on a wire rack.

Gingerbread

Gingerbread was a great favorite of the poet William Wordsworth.

---

2 1/4 cups flour
2 tsp ground ginger
pinch of ground cinnamon
1/2 cup butter
10 tbsp dark brown sugar
decorators' icing
a little water

Put the flour and spices into a mixing bowl and rub in the butter, using your fingertips, until the mixture resembles fine breadcrumbs. Stir in the sugar, using a little water, and mix to a firm dough. Press firmly into a parchment-lined and lightly greased square pan (the mixture should be about 1/2 inch thick). Bake at 325°F for about 30 minutes. Remove from the oven and cool on a wire rack, then cut into fingers.

To make gingerbread men, make as above, but roll out on a lightly floured board to about 1/4 inch thick, and using a gingerbread man cutter, cut out the figures. Place on a greased baking sheet and bake for about 15–20 minutes. When cooked, cool on a wire rack and use a pastry bag to pipe on the faces and buttons with decorators' icing.

Farmhouse Fruit Cake

Whole wheat flour is used in this cake, which gives it a distinctive nutty flavor. A nice thick slab, served with a piping hot mug of tea at a scrubbed pine table in a farmhouse kitchen, has to be simple fare at its best.

---

1 cup butter or margarine, softened
1 cup brown sugar
4 eggs
3 1/2 cups whole wheat self-rising flour
2 tsp mixed fruit cake spice (cinnamon, cloves, nutmeg)
grated rind of an orange
grated rind of a lemon
4 cups mixed dried fruit
1/2 cup glacé cherries
1 cup chopped nuts
2 tbsp sherry

Beat the butter and sugar together in a large mixing bowl until pale and creamy. Beat in the eggs, one at a time, adding a tablespoon of flour with each egg. Beat in the mixed spice, orange, and lemon rinds. Fold in the remaining flour with the fruit, cherries, and nuts, and stir in the sherry to give a smooth dropping consistency. Spoon the mixture into a parchment-lined and greased 8-inch round cake pan, and level the top of the cake with a metal spatula knife.

Bake for 2–3 hours at 300°F until golden brown and firm to touch. Leave to cool in the pan before turning out.

Marika's Marmalade Cake

This delicious cake was created by the late Marika Hanbury Tenison, who was one of England's most loved and respected cookery writers. Marika would have been the first person to admit that cakes and baking were not a part of cookery that she really enjoyed, but needs be. One afternoon she had unexpected visitors for tea at her beautiful seventeenth-century farmhouse on the top of Bodmin Moor in Cornwall. This cake was the end result of a mad dash to get a presentable tea together in the shortest possible time.

$2^1/_4$ cups self-rising flour
10 tbsp brown sugar
8 tbsp butter
2 large eggs
3 tbsp marmalade
3 tbsp cider (or apple juice)
1 cup mixed dried fruit
$^1/_4$ cup glacé cherries

This cake can be mixed in a food processor, or you can use an electric mixer. Put the flour, sugar, butter, and eggs into the processor and mix until you have a nice smooth dough, then add the marmalade and cider and process again. Add the fruit and glacé cherries and just process to mix. Put the mixture into a greased and parchment-lined loaf pan and bake for 1 hour at 350°F. When the cake is ready, leave it in the pan for 15–20 minutes before turning it out on a wire rack to cool.

Victoria Sponge

Named after Queen Victoria, this is a delicious light-as-air sponge made in two layers and sandwiched together with a filling of raspberry jam and buttercream.

$^{3}/_{4}$ cup butter
$^{3}/_{4}$ cup superfine sugar
3 eggs
1 $^{1}/_{2}$ cups self-rising flour
a little confectioners' sugar for topping
Filling:
$^{2}/_{3}$ cup butter
$^{3}/_{4}$ cup confectioners' sugar
2 tbsp warm water
3 tbsp jam

Line with parchment and lightly grease two 7-inch round cake pans. Beat the butter and sugar together in a bowl until pale and creamy. Beat in the eggs, one at a time, adding a tablespoon of flour with each egg. Fold in the remaining flour. Divide the mixture equally between the two pans and bake at 350°F for about 20 minutes until well risen, golden brown, and firm to touch in the center. Remove from the oven and allow to cool for about 10 minutes before turning out onto a wire cooling rack. To make the buttercream, soften the butter, gradually beat in the sugar, and finally beat in the water.

Spread the base of one cake with the jam, then carefully spread the buttercream over the jam. Place the other cake, base down, on top, and press down lightly. Sprinkle a little more confectioners' sugar on top.

Rich Chocolate Cake

1 3/4 cups self-rising flour	3/4 cup superfine sugar
2 tbsp cocoa powder	1 tbsp rum
6 tbsp each water/oil	2 large eggs, separated

Filling:

6 tbsp butter	2 tbsp warm water
3/4 cup confectioners' sugar, sifted	a few drops vanilla extract

Icing:

2 tsp cocoa powder
warm water
1/2 cup confectioners' sugar

Put the flour, cocoa, water, oil, superfine sugar, rum, and egg yolks into a large mixing bowl and beat well with a wooden spoon. Whisk the egg whites until stiff and then, using a metal spoon, fold into the chocolate mixture. Divide the mixture between two 8-inch round cake pans and bake at 350°F for about 35 minutes. Remove from the oven and cool on a wire rack.

To make the filling, beat the butter and sifted confectioners' sugar together with a tablespoon or two of warm water and one or two drops of vanilla extract until smooth. Use to sandwich the two cakes together.

To make the icing, dissolve the cocoa in a tablespoon of warm water. Sift the confectioners' sugar into a bowl and beat in the cocoa mixture, adding a little more warm water. The icing should only be thick enough to coat the back of a spoon. When the right consistency has been achieved, spread the icing on top.

Index